Did Y...

LINCO

A MISCELLANY

Compiled by Julia Skinner

With particular reference to the work of
Martin Andrew and Malcolm Knapp

THE FRANCIS FRITH COLLECTION

www.francisfrith.com

First published in the United Kingdom in 2010 by The Francis Frith Collection®

This edition published exclusively for Identity Books in 2010 ISBN 978-1-84589-520-4

Text and Design copyright The Francis Frith Collection®
Photographs copyright The Francis Frith Collection® except where indicated.

The Frith® photographs and the Frith® logo are reproduced under licence from
Heritage Photographic Resources Ltd, the owners of the Frith® archive and trademarks.
'The Francis Frith Collection', 'Francis Frith' and 'Frith' are registered trademarks of
Heritage Photographic Resources Ltd.

All rights reserved. No photograph in this publication may be sold to a third party other than in the original
form of this publication, or framed for sale to a third party. No parts of this publication may be reproduced,
stored in a retrieval system, or transmitted, in any form, or by any means, electronic, mechanical, photocopying,
recording or otherwise, without the prior permission of the publishers and copyright holder.

British Library Cataloguing in Publication Data

Did You Know? Lincolnshire - A Miscellany
Compiled by Julia Skinner
With particular reference to the work of Martin Andrew and Malcolm Knapp

The Francis Frith Collection
Frith's Barn, Teffont,
Salisbury, Wiltshire SP3 5QP
Tel: +44 (0) 1722 716 376
Email: info@francisfrith.co.uk
www.francisfrith.com

Printed and bound in Malaysia

Front Cover: **STAMFORD, GEORGE HOTEL 1922** 72305p

The colour-tinting is for illustrative purposes only, and is not intended to be historically accurate

AS WITH ANY HISTORICAL DATABASE, THE FRANCIS FRITH ARCHIVE IS CONSTANTLY BEING
CORRECTED AND IMPROVED, AND THE PUBLISHERS WOULD WELCOME INFORMATION ON
OMISSIONS OR INACCURACIES

CONTENTS

INTRODUCTION

After the end of the Roman occupation of Britain the area now known as Lincolnshire became a political entity for the first time, as the Anglian kingdom of Lindsey; the kingdom was absorbed into Mercia not long after AD700. Being on the east coast, and with the Trent and Witham highly navigable, the area was highly vulnerable to the longship-borne marauding armies of Danes (or Vikings), who are first recorded in the chronicles as ravaging the area in AD839. After the Peace of Wedmore of AD886 between the Anglo-Saxon King Alfred the Great and the Danish leader Guthram, England was divided up into two halves; the southern half remained under Anglo-Saxon rule, and the other became the 'Danelaw', which was under Danish control. Two of the important 'Five Boroughs' of the Danelaw were in Lincolnshire, the settlements of Stamford and Lincoln (the other three were Derby, Nottingham and Leicester). English re-conquest under King Edward the Elder ended Danish rule by AD920, but the Danish period of rule over Lincolnshire is recalled in hundreds of Danish place names around the county, particularly those ending in '-by', '-toft', '-thorpe' and '-ness'.

Lincolnshire is often dismissed as being wholly flat, but in fact the highest point on the railway line between London (King's Cross) and Edinburgh on the East Coast Main Line is actually in the county, just south of Grantham. Admittedly the whole of the south-east of the county is mostly flat land, with drains, dykes and canalised rivers and settlements along banks or on knolls that rise a mere few feet above the surrounding drained marshes or fens. However, this produces vast skies with towering clouds and long views of the higher land beyond, and the county's magnificent buildings thus assume greater significance. Who can forget their first long views of Lincoln Cathedral's three great towers atop the limestone ridge where the River Witham cuts through it, the setting sun bathing the towers and the clouds in roseate light, or the Boston Stump, that sublime church, seen from the Spalding direction, or even Tattershall Castle's medieval brick keep?

TATTERSHALL, THE CASTLE 1893 32081

LINCOLNSHIRE DIALECT WORDS

'Chunter' - to complain.

'Frim folk' - people from other area.

'Gimmer' - a ewe (female sheep) which has never given birth.

'Jiffle' - fidget.

'Kecks' - trousers.

'Kelch' - mud.

'Mardy' - bad tempered, sulky.

'Proggle' - to poke about (with a stick).

'Reasty' - rancid.

'Starnil' - a starling.

'Throng' - busy.

'Uneppen' - clumsy.

'Wassack' or 'Gump' - a fool.

'Wick' - lively.

'Yucker' - a young person.

'Yellowbelly' - the term used for someone born and bred in Lincoln. There are many theories about the origin of the name, one being that it derives from the bright yellow waistcoat worn by the 10th Regiment of Foot, later The Lincolnshire Regiment.

'Molly Grime' - in the church at Glentham near Market Rasen is a stone effigy (actually a 14th-century sarcophagus lid) of Lady Anne Tournay, which used to be washed by seven old maids every Good Friday with water from a nearby well, a ceremony that may have represented the entombment of Christ. Each woman was paid a shilling for performing this duty, raised from rent paid on a piece of land. The practice ended in 1832, when the land was sold. The habit of washing holy images is said to have been referred to as 'malgraen' in the local dialect, which became corrupted to 'Molly's Grime', and at one time in the area a child with a dirty face was called a 'Molly Grime'.

SPALDING, IN THE BULB FIELDS c1955 S388193

HAUNTED LINCOLNSHIRE

One of Lincoln's many ghost stories is that of 'Clarke's Hound', a lurcher dog originally owned by a poacher called William Clarke who was sentenced to death for murdering a gamekeeper. Clarke was held in Lincoln Castle before his execution, after which his dog pined away and died. The dog's body was stuffed and is now on show in the castle, but its ghost is said to roam the area around the castle walls, looking for its master.

The gatehouse of Thornton Abbey near Grimsby is said to be haunted by the ghost of Sir Thomas de Grethem, a 14th-century abbot. He was put on trial for witchcraft, and then walled up alive in a secret chamber. In the 1830s workmen found his skeleton.

Gunby Hall between Spilsby and Burgh-le-Marsh is said to be haunted by two ghosts, although the event which inspired the ghost story actually occurred at Bratoft Castle, which used to stand nearby. The story goes that in the late 17th century Margaret, daughter of Sir William Massingberd, fell in love with one of her father's servants. When Sir William discovered their affair he shot the man dead. In 1698, filled with remorse for his act, Sir William had Bratoft Castle demolished and then built Gunby Hall to live in; the ghost of his daughter and her doomed lover are said to wander along the path beside the pond near Gunby Hall, which is now known as the Ghost Walk.

The Sun Inn at Saxilby is said to be haunted by the ghost of Tom Otter, who murdered Mary Kirkham in 1805. When Mary's body was found it was taken to the inn; her blood spilled on to the steps as she was carried inside, and for many years it could not be cleaned off. Tom was sentenced to death at a trial at the Sun Inn, and then hanged.

The Old Hall at Gainsborough is said to be haunted by two ghosts. One is a Grey Lady, said to be the shade of a girl from the time of the Wars of the Roses, who pined to death after being locked away by her family when she fell in love with a knight on the 'wrong' side of the conflict. The other is the shade of the Viking king Sweyn Forkbeard, whose forces invaded England in the early 11th century. Sweyn made Gainsborough his capital and died there in 1014. The legend tells that Sweyn was killed by the spear-wielding phantom of St Edmund, who had been murdered by Vikings a century and a half earlier; Sweyn's moaning spirit is said to haunt the Hall, which was built on the site of the earlier building in which he died.

GAINSBOROUGH, THE OLD HALL c1955 G145001

LINCOLNSHIRE MISCELLANY

Alford Mill is shown in photograph A209026, below. This is a beautifully proportioned six-storey, five-sail Lincolnshire ogee-capped windmill, which is located on the A1104 road. Built in 1813 by Sam Oxley, an Alford millwright, it is still in working order and is open to the public regularly. Lincolnshire once had over 700 windmills.

Lincolnshire is England's premier agricultural county, and as it is on the eastern side of the country, it is one of the driest – hence most of its flat, fertile land is used for arable farming. The usual crops are wheat, barley, potatoes, oil seed rape, linseed, peas and millions of cabbages, as well as cauliflowers and onions. Lincolnshire is also famous for growing spring bulbs and daffodils, especially around Spalding and Holbeach.

**ALFORD
THE MILL c1955**
A209026

SANDILANDS, THE CROOKED CHURCH c1955 S480042

At Sandilands, just south of Sutton-on-Sea, St Clement's parish church is Lincolnshire's very own Leaning Tower, doubtless owing to its sandy foundations having settled since it was built in 1819 (see photograph S480042, above).

The church at Great Ponton near Grantham bears an unusual weather-vane in the shape of a violin. The present version is a replica of the original which was placed there in the 17th century, paid for as a 'thank you' by a grateful fiddler who emigrated to America and made his fortune there after local villagers raised the money for his fare.

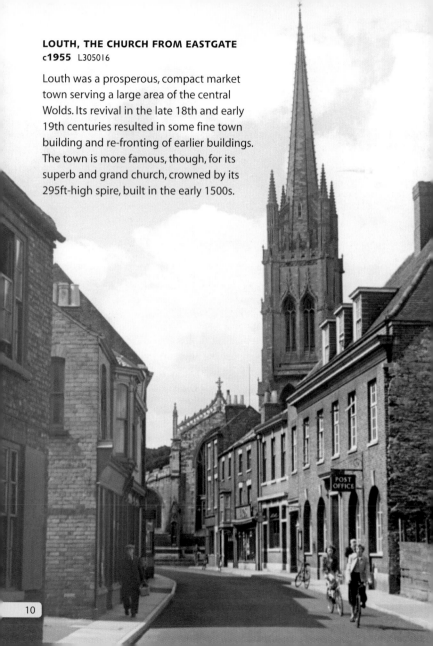

LOUTH, THE CHURCH FROM EASTGATE
c1955 L305016

Louth was a prosperous, compact market
town serving a large area of the central
Wolds. Its revival in the late 18th and early
19th centuries resulted in some fine town
building and re-fronting of earlier buildings.
The town is more famous, though, for its
superb and grand church, crowned by its
295ft-high spire, built in the early 1500s.

SPILSBY, THE FRANKLIN MONUMENT 1956 S391007

Dominating the Market Place of Spilsby is a bronze statue of Sir John Franklin, the Arctic explorer who was born in the town in 1786 (photograph S391007, above). His last expedition was to find the North-West Passage around the north of Canada, but Franklin and his crews died in 1847 when his ships, 'Erebus' and 'Terror', were trapped in the Arctic ice.

Many Lincolnshire men were involved in the exploration of Australia, including George Bass, surgeon of Boston (after whom the Bass Strait between Tasmania and south Australia is named), Matthew Flinders of Donington, and John Franklin of Spilsby, who sailed with Flinders (his uncle by marriage) as a young man when in 1801-02 he mapped the southern coast of Australia. Matthew Flinders named many places on the Eyre Peninsula of south Australia from Lincolnshire, such as Port Lincoln, Boston Island, Revesby Cove, and Cape Donington.

11

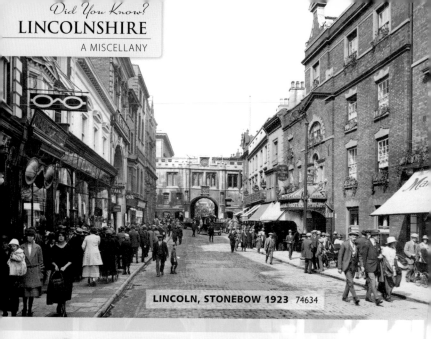

LINCOLN, STONEBOW 1923 74634

Lincoln was first established as a Roman legionary fortress and later became a Roman walled town, a 'colonia', or settlement for retired Roman legionaries. The area's earlier name, of Celtic-British origin, was 'Lindum', meaning 'a settlement by a pool, or lake', and the Roman town was known as 'Lindum Colonia'. In Anglo-Saxon times that name changed from 'Lindocolonia' to 'Lyndcylene', and then to Lincoln. Lincolnshire has the oldest canal in England, the 11-mile-long Fossdyke Navigation from Brayford Pool in Lincoln to the River Trent at Torksey, built by the Romans more than 1,800 years ago and still in use.

Medieval Lincoln produced a fine range of cloths; its best and most expensive was known as scarlet, but there was also blanket, which was white, and two varieties known as 'say'; grey and green. It is the green 'say' that is meant when we think of 'Lincoln green' today, usually in the context of Robin Hood and his Merry Men, who legend says dressed in 'Lincoln green' to camouflage themselves in Sherwood Forest.

The Lucy Tower in Lincoln Castle is named after Countess Lucy de Taillebois, who was Sheriff of Lincoln until her death in 1136. In the winter of 1140 Lucy's sons Ranulf and William involved Lincoln in the civil war between King Stephen and his cousin Matilda, when they seized control of the castle. Lincoln's citizens appealed to the king, who came with an army to besiege the fortress; it is said he attacked the castle by placing bowmen and siege engines on the west front of the cathedral. A relieving rebel army arrived in February 1141 and joined battle with the king's army, which was supported by the loyal inhabitants of the city. The king's troops were overwhelmed, and despite fighting heroically with a Danish battle-axe given to him by a Lincoln citizen, Stephen was captured. The short battle became known as the 'Joust of Lincoln'. In the aftermath the city was sacked by the rebel army and many inhabitants were killed.

LINCOLN, THE CASTLE 1890 25669

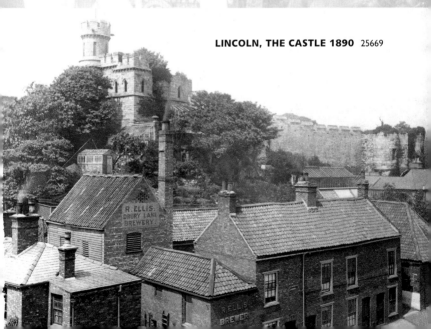

LINCOLN, AERIAL VIEW FROM THE SOUTH WEST c1960 L49088

Bishop Remigius started work on the cathedral at Lincoln in 1072. His west end was retained, altered and surmounted by towers raised by Bishop Alexander after a fire in 1141, but the rest of Alexander's work was replaced by the great Gothic church that we see today, a rebuild necessitated by an earthquake in 1185; from this tragedy one of Europe's most impressive cathedrals emerged, initially under St Hugh of Avalon, bishop from 1186 to 1200. His eastern transept and choir survive, but his east apse was replaced by the sublime Angel Choir, mainly to house his relics and accommodate pilgrims following his canonisation.

Now the headquarters of the Society for Lincolnshire History and Archaeology, the Jew's House at Lincoln dates from the 1170s and is one of the oldest houses in England (see photograph 25664, below). It was owned by a Jewess, Belaset, in the 1280s. It was a merchant's house, with shops on the ground floor and the hall and chamber on the upper floor; the hall was heated by a stone fireplace above the doorway.

LINCOLN, THE JEW'S HOUSE 1890 25664

After Lincoln Cathedral was partially destroyed by an earthquake in 1185, a plea was made for funds to help rebuild it. A poor man from Stow offered all his meagre savings to the project. Hearing of his generosity, Bishop Hugh noted that he would be rewarded in heaven where all were equal. To represent this, a statue of Bishop Hugh was placed on the pinnacle of the right-hand corner tower of the west front, while on the left-hand tower the Swineherd of Stow stands at exactly the same height.

Just outside the cathedral close in Lincoln is a statue of Alfred, Lord Tennyson, one of Lincolnshire's greatest sons, who was born in Somersby on the Wolds (see photograph 55109, opposite). The bronze statue shows Tennyson deep in thought, accompanied by his Siberian wolfhound, Karenina.

Lincoln's notable contribution to the First World War was the invention and manufacture of the armoured war machine known as the tank. First developed in 1915, the tank was put into full production the following year by Wm Foster Ltd at the New Wellington Works on New Boultham Road. In 1983 one of these first tanks returned to Lincoln. After restoration by Ruston's apprentices it was put on display at the Museum of Lincolnshire Life on Burton Road. Grantham was also involved in the history of the tank, as the track that enables tanks to move over difficult terrain was invented in the Grantham works of Richard Hornsby in the early 1900s.

The Anglo-Saxon freedom fighter against the Normans of the 11th century is famous as Hereward the Wake ('the watchful'), who came from a landowning family in Bourne in Lincolnshire. After the Norman invasion, Hereward's brother was killed at Bourne whilst protecting his family and estate, causing Hereward to take up arms in revenge. In 1069 he was party to the sacking of the Anglo-Saxon monastery at Peterborough, using the appointment of an unpopular Norman abbot as the excuse for doing this. Afterwards he took refuge in the Isle of Ely, where he held out for around three years. The Normans broke into Ely eventually, but Hereward managed to escape. What happened to him later is not known, but legend says that after his death he was buried in the abbey grounds at Crowland, in Lincolnshire.

November used to be the time when the ancient custom of bull running, or 'rebel's riot feast' took place in Stamford. This involved tormenting and chasing the unfortunate beast through the streets of the town, before it was slaughtered for the evening feast. The custom was banned in 1839, due as much to the cost of policing as to a more enlightened attitude towards animal rights.

Photograph 34831 (opposite) shows Croyland Abbey, which was built on the site of the 7th-century St Guthlac's timber hermitage at Crowland. In the Middle Ages Croyland was the richest abbey in Lincolnshire, but it is now only a fragment of its former glory: the nave north aisle is now the parish church with a monumental 15th-century tower capped by a squat spire. The remains of the rest of the abbey church are a tantalizing glimpse of an opulent past, while all the monastic buildings have now vanished.

**CROWLAND, CROYLAND ABBEY
1894** 34831

Lincolnshire possesses many Anglo-Saxon church towers – usually only the tower of the church was built in stone, as somewhere for local people to take refuge from Viking raids, whilst the rest of the church was wood – and St Peter's Church at Barton-upon-Humber (photograph B750016, below) is one of England's best, a national as well as a Lincolnshire treasure. Part of the church is Anglo-Saxon and the other is 13th-century; it was made redundant in 1972 and is now protected by English Heritage.

BARTON-UPON-HUMBER, ST PETER'S CHURCH c1955 B750016

STAMFORD, RED LION SQUARE 1922 72300

Stamford is one of England's most attractive and historic towns. An ancient trackway once crossed the River Welland by the stone ford that gave the town its name. In the period leading up to the Norman Conquest in 1066, Stamford became a centre for trade in a popular type of warm and close-woven cloth known as 'haberget', and also had a pottery industry whose wares graced medieval tables well into the 13th century. Stamford was the site of one of the major mints of Anglo-Saxon England, striking 10% of all the coins produced in the country. By medieval times Red Lion Square in Stamford had developed into the site of the town's sheep market. The large building which features prominently in photograph 72300 (above) as the Freeman, Hardy & Willis shoe shop is known to contain elements of a large 14th-century timber-framed building. It has been suggested that this may be the wool house of the Browns, one of the town's most successful families of wool merchants.

Much of 18th-century Stamford's trade came from its location on the Great North Road (now the A1), and it had numerous coaching inns such as the George Hotel, an inn since 1568 and once classed as the best hotel on the Great North Road. The George Hotel is noted for its 'gallows' sign spanning the road, which is still there, and is thought to be an attempt at curing instability in the front wall arising from when it was rebuilt in 1724.

In the days before tarmac the roads around Stamford were topped with limestone that made them dangerously slippery for cyclists, and cycle guides of the late 19th century wrote off this stretch of the Great North Road as being dangerously unrideable when wet.

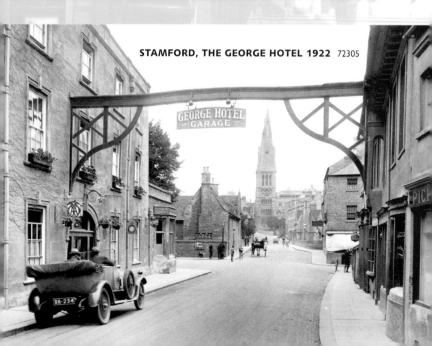

STAMFORD, THE GEORGE HOTEL 1922 72305

STAMFORD, BURGHLEY HOUSE 1922 72323A

The new graveyard of St Martin's Church in Stamford, off Barnack Road, is the final resting place of Daniel Lambert, who was the heaviest man in Britain at the time of his death, aged 39, in 1809. He weighed in at almost 53 stone. He died at the Waggon and Horses Inn whilst on a visit to Stamford races, and part of the inn had to be demolished to allow his coffin to be removed.

William Cecil, Secretary of State to Queen Elizabeth I, built the magnificent Burghley House near Stamford, between 1552 and 1587, as his country estate (see photograph 72323A, above). The interior was redesigned in the late 17th century and includes carving by Grinling Gibbons, plasterwork by Edward Martin and painting by Verrio.

The great expansion of Grantham came about during the Victorian era, following the success of Richard Hornsby's engineering works and the arrival of the railway in the mid 19th century. Grantham was founded by the Anglo-Saxons, probably in either the 6th or 7th century, and the boundaries of this earliest settlement are still to be found in the street layout and water courses of the town. It was later within the Danelaw, and there are still many reminders of Grantham's Danish heritage in some of the town's street name endings, such as Swinegate, Watergate and Westgate. The word 'gate' is a corruption of a Scandinavian word that means 'the way of' or 'the way to'. Thus Watergate means the way to the water, and Westgate means the way out of town to the west.

Grantham was the birthplace in 1925 of Margaret Thatcher, Britain's first woman Prime Minister. Her father ran a grocer's shop in North Parade in the town.

The south porch of St Wulfram's Church in Grantham contains one of the town's great treasures, the chained library. It was founded in 1598 by the Rev Francis Trigge, rector of the nearby village of Welbourn. The library was catalogued in 1988, and a total of 82 chained books were repaired and restored. The earliest is dated 1472; it is bound with two others dated 1476.

The expression 'Bomber County' was an apt description for Lincolnshire during the Second World War – at that time there were 46 aerodromes in the county, more than in any other, many of which saw much action as Wellington and Lancaster bombers took off on nightly raids. The headquarters of No 5 Group Bomber Command was located in Grantham for part of the war, and Air Marshall Sir Arthur Harris lived in the town for quite a time. In fact, the famous 617 Squadron 'Dambusters' raid was organised from Grantham, and launched from RAF Scampton in 1943.

GRANTHAM, THE GUILDHALL
1889 22286

It was some time soon after the diversion of the Great North Road to come through Grantham when the Angel Inn, as it was formerly named, was built. It is often stated that the inn was first built to be a Commandery of the Knights Templar, but Reverend B Street disputed this in his work 'Historical Notes on Grantham', (1857). He concluded from his research that the building did indeed belong to the Knights Templar, but was used by them as a hostel for travellers and pilgrims, rather than a Commandery, or Preceptory, of the Order. Reverend Street believed that the Angel later passed to the Knights Hospitallers, and became a useful haven for medieval travellers. The façade of the present-day building is of the mid 15th century, but the cellars could be earlier, and even original. The inn is considered to be one of the oldest inns in England, and as the Angel Inn was one of the numerous coaching inns in Grantham during the 18th and 19th centuries. A large extension was built behind the medieval façade in 1776 to cater for the busy stage coach trade – at this time, many coaches came through Grantham each day going to almost as many different destinations. The name of the inn was changed to the Angel and Royal Hotel in 1866 after a visit by the Prince of Wales, later Edward VII.

The earliest surviving part of the Angel and Royal Hotel building in Grantham is the main archway, carved with the heads of Edward III and Queen Philippa. The grand upper room is known as the Chambre du Roi, or the King's Room, and it was here in 1483 that Richard III heard of the treachery of the Duke of Buckingham and signed his death warrant. One of the many interesting stories about the inn concerns Michael Soloman, a one-time landlord, who died in 1706. In his will he left 40 shillings to be paid each Michaelmas Day for the preaching of a sermon against drunkenness – this custom endures to this day.

GRANTHAM, THE ANGEL
AND ROYAL HOTEL 1893
33257

Photograph G43051 (below) of the Beehive Inn shows one of the more unusual sights in Grantham; perched in the tree outside the inn is the 'living sign' of a real bee hive, which is still there, complete with a resident colony of honey bees. The pub itself is of great antiquity, and there has been a bee hive in a tree there since the early 1700s, but not the same one. The short poem on the sign attached to the wall of the pub reads:

> *Stop Traveller this wondrous sign explore,*
> *And say when thou hast viewed it o'er and o'er,*
> *Grantham now two rarities are thine,*
> *A lofty Steeple and a living sign.*

GRANTHAM, THE BEEHIVE INN c1955 G43051

SCUNTHORPE, HIGH STREET 1904 52160v

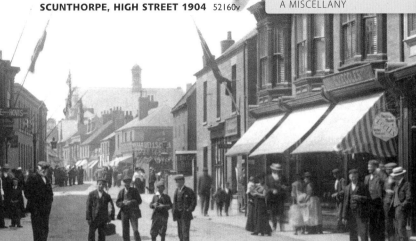

Scunthorpe is recorded in the Domesday Book as 'Escumetorp', which in Old Norse means 'Skuma's homestead'. The town lies on a rich bed of iron ore and limestone, making it a major steel manufacturing centre, although most economically viable seams have now been mined and raw materials are mostly imported nowadays. In February 2008 Scunthorpe and the surrounding area in north Lincolnshire was shaken by one of the most powerful earthquakes ever recorded in Britain; it lasted for 10 seconds, and measured 5.2 on the Richter scale.

In the 19th century a number of successful engineering firms were established around the county. Gainsborough had Marshall's, at the large Britannia Works; Grantham had Hornsby's; and Lincoln had Ruston's, Robey's and Clayton & Shuttleworth's. Clayton & Shuttleworth made highly efficient portable steam engines, which had a number of purposes, including the driving of farm machinery, and the company became the largest manufacturer of steam engines and threshing machines in Britain.

In the 16th century Henry VIII dissolved the monasteries, and 36 of the 52 monasteries in Lincolnshire had been closed by August 1536. This was highly unpopular with the ordinary people, and led to the 'Lincolnshire Rising'. It started in October 1536 in Louth, Horncastle and Caistor, from where people marched to Lincoln, gathering others from elsewhere in the county as they went. The worst incident was when Dr Raynes, Chancellor of Lincoln Cathedral, was dragged from Old Bolingbroke to Horncastle, and clubbed to death by the mob. The rebels were joined in Lincoln by a force from Boston, including some sympathetic members of the gentry, and sent a letter to the king listing their grievances. The king's reply was read out in the Chapter House of Lincoln Cathedral, in which he referred to the county of Lincolnshire as 'one of the most brute and beastly in the realm'. On the following day the gentry amongst the rebels decided to capitulate to the king's forces sent to Lincoln, and advised the ordinary people to go home, but Henry VIII was determined to make an example of Lincolnshire, and a number of the rebels were hanged.

The Old Hall at Gainsborough (see photograph G145001, on page 7) is a 15th-century timber-framed manor house which contains the most complete medieval kitchen in the country and has a magnificent single-arched braced roof in its main hall. In the 16th century it was the home of Henry VIII's sixth wife, Katherine Parr, when she was married to her first husband, Edward de Burgh, second Baron Borough of Gainsborough.

The fashion for sea bathing began to catch on in Lincolnshire around the turn of the 18th and 19th centuries, mainly amongst the wealthier classes, and Lincolnshire squires and their families drove to Skegness, Mablethorpe and Freiston Shore to keep in the swing. The Skegness Inn (later the Vine Hotel) and the New Inn (Hildreds Hotel) and a number of lodging houses in Skegness catered for the visitors, but it was only when the railway arrived in 1873 that the resort of Skegness really took off. Almost all the land and farm holdings in Skegness belonged to the Earl of Scarbrough, and with the coming of the railway Lord Scarbrough decided to develop Skegness as a model watering place. Work began in 1877, and the next five years saw the tiny coastal village overlaid with wide tree-lined avenues, a new main street, promenades and villas, homes and lodging houses to suit all classes. New residents began pouring in to open businesses or work on the construction.

After the railway arrived in Skegness in 1873 the Great Northern Railway began running Sunday excursions from the towns and cities of the East Midlands, especially Nottingham. Skegness was promoted by the well-known jolly fisherman poster and the slogan 'Skegness is so Bracing'. Bracing is a good word to describe the north and east winds that frequently blow into the coast here, but the sandy beaches are superb compensation. The resort was very much developed with day trips and excursions in mind; in photograph 62843 (below) we can see the funfair actually on the sands above the high water mark, including a helter-skelter tower.

SKEGNESS, FROM THE PIER 1910 62843

SKEGNESS, THE PIER 1904 51763

In 1881 Skegness acquired a splendid pier, seen in photograph 51763 (above) as it was in 1904, in a form unrecognisable to the modern visitor. Seaside piers were a Victorian creation, but Skegness and Cleethorpes were the only resorts on the Lincolnshire coast to boast such a prestigious amenity. The pier at Cleethorpes had opened eight years earlier, but the Skegness structure was half as long again as its rival's, and at 1,817 feet it was claimed to be the fourth longest in the country. In 1978 the section of the pier between the concert hall and the end was destroyed in storms. The landward end of the 1840-foot-long pier had already been submerged in 1970 by the enclosed Skegness Pier Amusements, although some of the original structure can be seen at the sea end.

Richard Hudson moved to Skegness with his wife and children in 1878. He and his forebears were well-known musicians in his native Preston, and he opened a music shop in the High Street. One of his sons, George Hudson, established himself as a maker of fine violins, violas and violincellos, which are now collectors' items. Most of these instruments were made at Pier View, which was trademarked as 'The Cremona Workshop'. Another musician who worked in Skegness, playing his trombone in the pier orchestra, was the English composer Gustav Holst, born in Cheltenham in 1874. It is recorded that 'he scored his Cotswold Symphony in his free time on the sands' whilst he was living and working in the town.

The name of Skegness means Skeggi's 'ness', or headland, and derives from the time when this part of England was settled and controlled by the Danes, but it was a haven town even earlier, in Roman times. The Skegness that was known to the Romans and Danes was swept away by the tide in 1526 and lies under the sea perhaps three-quarters of a mile from the present shore.

Lumley Road and Lumley Square in Skegness were named after the Earl of Scarbrough's family name. Photograph 44354 (opposite) shows Lumley Road in 1899; on the left of the photograph is the Lion Hotel, which opened in 1881. A feature of the new hotel was the stone lion perched on the roof above the corner entrance, which was carved from sandstone by Richard Winn of Grimsby. The lion eventually became unsafe on the roof, and in 1904 it was brought down to stand on the pavement on the Roman Bank frontage. There it remained almost throughout the 20th century, to the great delight of thousands of small children who could never pass that point without demanding 'a ride on the lion'. This much loved local emblem disappeared shortly before J D Wetherspoon took over the Lion Hotel in 1997, when the new owners renamed the hotel the Red Lion.

SKEGNESS, LUMLEY ROAD 1899 44354

In 1927 Billy Butlin arrived in Skegness with a couple of living vans and three lorries packed with fairground equipment, and set up a funfair on the North Parade frontage. In 1928 Butlin set up a new funfair on the south side of the pier; the following summer he transferred his stalls and rides there, and Butlin's retained this big amusement park until 1964, when the tenancy was taken over by Botton Bros, who rebuilt the site from scratch. On the left of photograph 62846 (opposite) is the Osbert House Hotel in Skegness. Billy Butlin bought the Osbert House Hotel in the late 1930s and it became Butlin House, head office for all his holiday camps, hotels and amusement parks, which by then were spread across the country. The building was demolished in 1972.

Butlin's holiday camp at Ingoldmells, near Skegness, built in 1936, was the first holiday camp in Britain. Locals were surprised during the Second World War when it was claimed in a broadcast by Lord Haw Haw, Hitler's propagandist, to have been sunk during the war; at that time it was the Royal Navy training camp HMS 'Royal Arthur'. Today, the idea of spending a holiday at a post-war Butlin's is not attractive. The chalets were arranged in straight lines, as in a military camp, and there were barbed-wire fences and communal bathrooms. Constant instruction blared out from the tannoy system: get up; queue for breakfast; go to the lido; buy an ice cream; don't forget the three-legged race – and so on, right through until bed time. But everyone had an unforgettable time.

SKEGNESS, GRAND PARADE AND THE CLOCK TOWER 1910 62846

Boston is named after its parish church, dedicated to the Saxon monk St Botolph. The town was called 'St Botolph's' or 'Botolph's Town' until about 1400, but since then the shorter name 'Boston' has been used. Boston was laid out along the banks of the River Witham c1100 and rapidly became a great port. It acquired town walls in 1285, and in 1353 it wrested away Lincoln's wool staple. It was the wool trade that built the town – in the Middle Ages, fairs were trading events to which people came long distances to buy and sell goods, and Boston Fair was one of the main places in England where wool was bought and sold. The largest producers of wool in the Middle Ages included the Cistercian abbeys of Yorkshire and Lincolnshire, and they and other monasteries acquired houses in Boston that they could use when they came to sell their wool at the fair – the name of Fountain Lane in Boston still indicates the part of Wormgate where Fountains Abbey owned several buildings.

BOSTON, THE RIVER VIEW 1890 26067

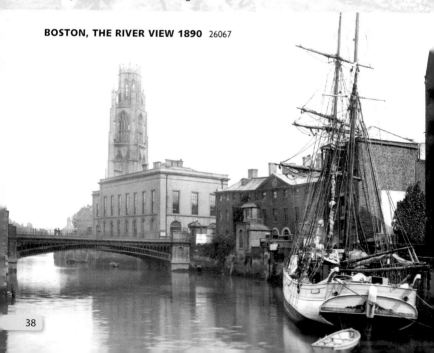

BOSTON, ST BOTOLPH'S CHURCH, THE CHOIR EAST 1892 32070a

Boston's town centre is dominated by its large triangular market place and the mighty tower of St Botolph's Church, universally known as the Boston Stump (seen in the background of photograph 26067, opposite). Crowned by a superb octagonal lantern complete with pinnacles and flying buttresses, it soars 272 feet above the town and can be seen from miles around; it used to serve as a landmark for shipping, for the lantern once used to have a beacon lit in it at night.

The interior of St Botolph's Church at Boston (photograph 32070a, above) is a magnificent example of the Decorated period, with the nave arcades and vaulted roof leading the eye to the soaring chancel arch and the vast east window. In the chancel the original 14th-century choir stalls survive, along with 62 wonderful carved misericords (small wooden seats); the carvings include a monk thrashing a boy, a bear playing an organ, a mermaid and sailors, and a virgin and a unicorn.

Boston became prosperous in the Middle Ages, and the local merchants founded guilds and friaries and started the construction of the great parish church that still dominates the town. Medieval guilds were predominantly religious bodies with a strong social element. St Mary's Guild, formed in 1260, was the first guild in Boston, and for nearly 300 years was the main power in the town. Its hall was rebuilt in the 1390s, and is still in use as the town's museum. A number of other Guilds followed, including the Corpus Christi Guild founded in 1335 – its hall was near the river and might be the timber-framed building in South Street now called Shodfriars Hall (see photograph 22274, below).

BOSTON, SHODFRIAR'S HALL 1889 22274

In the early 17th century some Protestants who followed an extreme form of worship, known as Puritans, felt that they were being persecuted and decided to leave the country to be free to worship in the way they wanted. A group from north Nottinghamshire, including William Brewster and William Bradford, tried to leave England in 1607, catching a boat from a creek downstream of Boston in an attempt to sail to the Netherlands. They were betrayed and captured, and put on trial in the court in Boston's Guildhall (photograph 32073, on page 43); the cells that briefly held them can still be seen. The dissenters later sailed from Immingham to the Netherlands and in 1620 some of them, known as the Pilgrim Fathers, made their famous voyage to Massachusetts on the 'Mayflower' – including William Brewster and William Bradford, who had been previously detained in Boston.

Union Street and Union Place in Boston are so called because they were built about the same time as the Act of Union of 1800, which abolished the Irish Parliament and included Ireland in the United Kingdom.

Boston became famous as a centre of Protestantism in the first half of the 17th century. From 1612 to 1633 the vicar was the zealous John Cotton, who attracted many people to the town with his powerful preaching. In 1627 a more intense persecution of Puritan 'religious extremists' began, and in 1629 the Massachusetts Bay Company was formed, a group of people who planned to move to America to find religious freedom; the company's leadership was based in the area around Boston, and at the heart of the planned emigration was the household of Theophilus Clinton-Fiennes, the 4th Earl of Lincoln, who was a follower of Reverend Cotton. The earl's main home was Tattershall Castle but he also had a house in Boston. Among the leaders of the group were Thomas Dudley (who lived in Boston and was Lord Lincoln's steward) and his son-in-law Simon Bradstreet. The first fleet from Boston sailed to the New World in 1630. One ship carried the Rev Isaac Johnson and his wife, a sister of Lord Lincoln, and was renamed 'Arbella' in her honour. Also on that ship were Thomas Dudley and his daughter, Anne Bradstreet, who was to be the first American poet to have her work published. In 1633 Boston's Puritan vicar, the Reverend John Cotton himself, and several more families of his congregation sailed to New England in the 'Griffin'. It is estimated that 250 of the 3,000 people then living in Boston emigrated to New England before 1640, and men from Boston held one or other of the top jobs in the colony for the next 60 years; the settlement of 'Boston' in Massachusetts was named after the Lincolnshire town from which these leaders came.

The dual-carriageway known as John Adams Way in Boston is named after the second president of the USA. John Adams was a lawyer in Boston, Massachusetts at the time of the American Revolution and a champion of liberty. His connection with Boston in Lincolnshire is that his wife's ancestors (named Quincy) came from this area. His eldest son, John Quincy Adams, became the sixth president of the USA in 1825.

BOSTON, THE GUILDHALL 1893
32073

A single-track railway built in 1863 turned Cleethorpes into a welcoming seaside town. Cleethorpes could boast several miles of unspoilt beaches and, in 1873, a pier, which when first built was much longer than it is now. Originally 1,200 foot in length, the pier was a huge tourist attraction, and was so long that its far end used to be in the water even at low tide, making it a delight for land-based sea fishermen. A pier head concert hall was built in 1888, but it was destroyed by fire in 1903. A new pavilion was built nearer to the promenade in 1906, which remains today. During the Second World War it was feared that the pier presented an easy access point for sea-borne invaders from Germany – they might be able to alight from ships or U-boats without entering inshore waters – so a middle section of the pier was removed, reducing the length of the part attached to land to just 355 feet. When the war ended, the Government was unable to fund a replacement middle section, so the isolated seaward section was demolished. Some of the salvaged material from the demolition of the seaward part of Cleethorpes Pier was used on Leicester City Football Club's new Filbert Street stand.

By the 1920s Grimsby was the largest fishing port in the world, and a huge tonnage of cod, haddock and herring from the North Sea and the Icelandic fishing grounds was processed in the town. During the inter-war years there was exceptional growth of the steam trawler fleets based in both Hull and Grimsby, and from this time until the mid 1970s Grimsby provided one fifth of all the fish consumed in the UK. The decline in the industry came as a result of the fishing limitations that Iceland placed on the fishing grounds which led to the 'cod wars' of the 1970s, resulting in a huge decline in fish landings and the eventual loss of the deep sea trawling fleet. Fortunately though, Grimsby people adapt. Smaller shallow-water seine fishermen took over, and with a substantial fresh fish processing and cold storage facility in town, fish was still brought overland to Grimsby for sale and processing. The National Fishing Heritage Centre opened at the Alexandra Dock at Grimsby in 1991, and the trawler 'Ross Tiger' which is moored outside the centre is a reminder of the proud fishing heritage that built the town.

GRIMSBY, THE ROYAL DOCK c1955 G60019

A carved stone bust of Gervase Holles, former mayor and Grimsby MP, can be seen on the outside of Grimsby's Town Hall. This renowned historian became Mayor of Grimsby in 1640, and was a patriot and a royalist, supporting Charles I during the Civil War. Many of his manuscripts were destroyed, but among those remaining is the Grimsby Magna, a fascinating history of medieval Grimsby.

Photograph G60703 (opposite) shows a modern statue in the grounds of Grimsby College of Technology. The statue features a young boy, Havelok, being carried on the shoulders of Grim the fisherman, a scene from 'The Lay of Havelok the Dane'. This tells how Havelok, the orphaned son of the King of Denmark, was cast adrift on the sea by his evil guardian. A raft bore the child to the coast of Lincolnshire where he was found by Grim, the legendary founder of Grimsby, who brought him up as his own son. When he grew up Havelok discovered the truth about his birth and returned to his homeland, eventually becoming King of Denmark. During his youth Havelok became renowned for his feats of strength. He once went to the court of Alsi, the King of Lindsey, at Lincoln, where he worked in the royal kitchens. King Alsi had promised his daughter Goldburga to the strongest and fairest man in the land. At a stone-throwing contest Havelok managed to lift one great stone higher and hurl it further than anyone else, and thus won the hand of his wife. Local legend says that the Havelok Stone outside the Welholme Gallery in Grimsby is the stone reputedly thrown by him to win the hand of Goldburga!

By 2003, Grimsby was officially Britain's luckiest lottery town, with eleven major wins in the area since the first draw in 1994. Individual wins of £14 million, £8 million and £3 million alone have helped earn Grimsby the nickname of 'Winsby', and experts believe that the population of approx 110,000 is two-and-a-half times more likely to land a fortune than that of the rest of Britain.

GRIMSBY, THE STATUE OF GRIM 2004 G60703

SPORTING LINCOLNSHIRE

Annual horse racing events in Lincoln began in 1680 and continued on Lincoln Heath until 1773, after which they were relocated to the West Commons. In time the races became a regular three-day meeting held each spring. The most celebrated race was the Lincolnshire Handicap, first run in 1849; the Lincoln races came to an end in 1964 but the 'Lincoln Handicap', as it is now known, still takes place each spring, although it has been transferred to Doncaster racecourse where it remains central to the flat-racing calendar, being the opening race of the season.

Lincoln City FC are nicknamed 'the Imps', but do you know the name of their female counterparts, Lincoln City LFC? The answer is – 'The Lady Imps'.

Paul Palmer, the British swimmer who won the silver medal in the 400 metres Freestyle event at the 1996 Olympics in Atlanta, USA, was born in Lincoln in 1974. He attended Lincoln Christ's Hospital School, and trained at the City of Lincoln Pentaqua Swimming Club.

The nickname of Grimsby Town FC is the Mariners. For many years, a favourite quiz question in English football trivia was 'Which league football team play all their games away from home?'. The answer was Grimsby Town, whose home stadium of Blundell Park is in the neighbouring borough of Cleethorpes, but this is no longer a unique situation, as several teams have shared a ground during the building of new stadiums.

Grimsby's sporting heroes include cross-channel record-breaking swimmer Brenda Fisher; the former British number one-ranked tennis star Shirley Bloomer, who married the athlete Chris Brasher; the former top-ranked snooker players Mike Hallett and Dean Reynolds.

Boston Rowing Club hosts the Boston Rowing Marathon each year. It is a long-distance race of 49 kilometres (31 miles), whose length makes it unique in Britain. The course of the race is along the River Witham from Lincoln to Boston, starting at Brayford Pool in Lincoln and finishing at the Boston clubhouse. Crews from all over the UK compete in the marathon, which can take up to six hours to finish – the current record of 2 hours 59 minutes and 45 seconds was set in 1991, by a University of London eight.

QUIZ QUESTIONS

Answers on page 52.

1. Which royal mistress and ancestress of the present royal family is buried in Lincoln Cathedral?

2. According to Lincolnshire folklore, what does it mean if a baby is born with exceptionally large ears?

3. Where will you find the Lincoln Imp, and what is it?

4. One of the most famous men in the field of science and mathematics was born in 1643 at Woolsthorpe Manor in Woolsthorpe-by-Colsterworth in Lincolnshire, and went to school in Grantham – who was he?

5. Whose statue stands outside the Associated British Ports offices beside Grimsby Docks?

6. It is often said that Boston Stump, the tower of the parish church of St Botolph in Boston, is 'built on wool'. What does this mean?

7. Which international festival is held on Cleethorpes Beach each year?

8. Which animals kept on the Lincolnshire fens around Boston were referred to as 'the fenman's treasurer'?

9. How is it now possible to visit an old Stamford shop in the city of York?

10. The armoured fighting vehicle known as the tank was invented and produced in Lincolnshire during the First World War, at the New Wellington Works of Wm Foster Ltd in Lincoln. But why were these vehicles called 'tanks'?

RECIPE

LINCOLN GINGER BISCUITS

350g/12oz self-raising flour
225g/8oz sugar
2 teaspoonfuls bicarbonate of soda
115g/4oz butter or margarine
2 teaspoonfuls ground ginger
2 teaspoonfuls golden syrup
1 beaten egg

Pre-heat the oven to 180°C/350°F/Gas Mark 4.

Place all the dry ingredients in a bowl. Heat the butter or margarine and golden syrup gently in a pan until the fat has melted, then pour over the dry ingredients and mix to a fairly stiff consistency, whilst slowly adding in the beaten egg. Roll small pieces of the dough in your hand to make balls about the size of a walnut.

Place each ball of dough on a greased baking sheet, making sure they are well spaced apart. Bake for 15-20 minutes in the pre-heated oven until the biscuits are golden brown.

RECIPE

LINCOLNSHIRE PLUM BREAD

This is especially good if the dried fruit is soaked overnight in cold (milk-less) tea before cooking.

450g/1 lb plain flour (strong bread-making flour is best)
225g/8oz prunes, cut into small pieces
115ml/4fl oz milk, warmed
115g/4oz butter, melted
4 tablespoonfuls caster sugar
50g/2oz currants
50g/2oz sultanas
15g/ 1/2 oz easy-blend dried yeast
2 eggs, lightly beaten
1 teaspoonful ground cinnamon
1 teaspoonful ground allspice
1 pinch of salt

Mix together the warmed milk, sugar, butter, yeast, beaten egg, salt, and spices. Add the flour, and beat the mixture until it is smooth, to make soft pliable dough. Turn out the dough onto a floured surface, and knead it until it is smooth and elastic. Place the dough in a bowl, cover, and allow the bowl to stand in a warm place until the dough has doubled in size. Knock back the dough and knead it again briefly, adding the dried fruit and making sure that it is evenly distributed. Divide the dough into two pieces, and place into two 450g (1 lb) greased and lined loaf tins. Cover and leave again in a warm place rise until doubled in size.

Pre-heat the oven to 190°C/375°F/Gas Mark 5. Place the loaf tins on a pre-heated baking sheet and bake for 40-50 minutes, then remove the loaves from the tins and return them to the oven to cook for a further 5-10 minutes, or until they sound hollow when tapped on the base. Store the loaves in an airtight container and serve in slices, spread with butter. This also makes excellent toast.

QUIZ ANSWERS

1. Katherine Swynford, the mistress of John of Gaunt (one of the sons of Edward III), and mother to four of his children; the couple eventually married. One of the children was John Beaufort, from whom all of England's succeeding royal families can be traced. She died in 1405, and her story inspired Anya Seton's famous historical novel 'Katherine'.

2. It was an old Lincolnshire belief that when a baby was born with noticeably large ears, it was a sign that he or she would be successful in life.

3. The Lincoln Imp is a stone carving in the form of a small diabolical creature in Lincoln Cathedral. The builders of the shrine of St Hugh wanted pilgrims to have in mind the ever-present danger of evil, so they included a reminder of the devil high up between two arches on the north side of the Angel Choir.

4. Sir Isaac Newton. The young Isaac attended the Old School at Grantham in the early 1600s and carved his name on one of its window sills, which can still be seen. In later life, it was at his home of Woolsthorpe Manor near Grantham that he is said to have watched an apple fall to the ground and begun to understand the law of gravity. An imposing statue of Sir Isaac Newton stands on what is now known as St Peter's Hill in Grantham, which was erected in 1857. The War Office donated the bronze for the statue from Russian cannons captured during the Crimean War.

5. Prince Albert, husband of Queen Victoria, who laid the foundation stone of the new Royal Dock in 1852.

6. Some people think that is said that the Boston Stump is 'built on wool' because sacks of wool were thrown into the foundation pit when the tower was built. This is not so. In fact, it means that the tower was paid for from the profits made by the merchants importing and exporting wool and other goods through the medieval port of Boston.

7. The International Kite Flying Festival.

8. Geese, valued for their meat, feathers and quills. Geese were bred on the Lincolnshire fens in great numbers and their feathers were plucked twice a year to fill feather beds and pillows. In the 19th and 20th centuries, Boston was the centre of the fenland feather industry, with several factories purifying feathers for pillows and other purposes. Now the only business left in this industry is Fogarty's, which also uses man-made fillers.

9. Grant's the butchers' shop which formerly stood in Stamford's High Street was dismantled in 1936 and moved to the York Castle Museum, where it was reconstructed to form part of the museum's famous Victorian street scene, 'Kirkgate'.

10. Tanks are so called because the workmen who built the hulls of the first vehicles during the First World War were told that they were building tracked water containers or 'water tanks' for the army, in order for the production of these new fighting vehicles to be kept secret.

FRANCIS FRITH

PIONEER VICTORIAN PHOTOGRAPHER

Francis Frith, founder of the world-famous photographic archive, was a complex and multi-talented man. A devout Quaker and a highly successful Victorian businessman, he was philosophical by nature and pioneering in outlook. By 1855 he had already established a wholesale grocery business in Liverpool, and sold it for the astonishing sum of £200,000, which is the equivalent today of over £15,000,000. Now in his thirties, and captivated by the new science of photography, Frith set out on a series of pioneering journeys up the Nile and to the Near East.

INTRIGUE AND EXPLORATION

He was the first photographer to venture beyond the sixth cataract of the Nile. Africa was still the mysterious 'Dark Continent', and Stanley and Livingstone's historic meeting was a decade into the future. The conditions for picture taking confound belief. He laboured for hours in his wicker dark-room in the sweltering heat of the desert, while the volatile chemicals fizzed dangerously in their trays. Back in London he exhibited his photographs and was 'rapturously cheered' by members of the Royal Society. His reputation as a photographer was made overnight.

VENTURE OF A LIFE-TIME

By the 1870s the railways had threaded their way across the country, and Bank Holidays and half-day Saturdays had been made obligatory by Act of Parliament. All of a sudden the working man and his family were able to enjoy days out, take holidays, and see a little more of the world.

With typical business acumen, Francis Frith foresaw that these new tourists would enjoy having souvenirs to commemorate their days out. For the next thirty years he travelled the country by train and by pony and trap, producing fine photographs of seaside resorts and beauty spots that were keenly bought by millions of Victorians. These prints were painstakingly pasted into family albums and pored over during the dark nights of winter, rekindling precious memories of summer excursions. Frith's studio was soon supplying retail shops all over the country, and by 1890 F Frith & Co had become the greatest specialist photographic publishing company in the world, with over 2,000 sales outlets, and pioneered the picture postcard.

FRANCIS FRITH'S LEGACY

Francis Frith had died in 1898 at his villa in Cannes, his great project still growing. By 1970 the archive he created contained over a third of a million pictures showing 7,000 British towns and villages.

Frith's legacy to us today is of immense significance and value, for the magnificent archive of evocative photographs he created provides a unique record of change in the cities, towns and villages throughout Britain over a century and more. Frith and his fellow studio photographers revisited locations many times down the years to update their views, compiling for us an enthralling and colourful pageant of British life and character.

We are fortunate that Frith was dedicated to recording the minutiae of everyday life. For it is this sheer wealth of visual data, the painstaking chronicle of changes in dress, transport, street layouts, buildings, housing and landscape that captivates us so much today, offering us a powerful link with the past and with the lives of our ancestors.

Computers have now made it possible for Frith's many thousands of images to be accessed almost instantly. The archive offers every one of us an opportunity to examine the places where we and our families have lived and worked down the years. Its images, depicting our shared past, are now bringing pleasure and enlightenment to millions around the world a century and more after his death.

For further information visit: www.francisfrith.com

INTERIOR DECORATION

Frith's photographs can be seen framed and as giant wall murals in thousands of pubs, restaurants, hotels, banks, retail stores and other public buildings throughout Britain. These provide interesting and attractive décor, generating strong local interest and acting as a powerful reminder of gentler days in our increasingly busy and frenetic world.

FRITH PRODUCTS

All Frith photographs are available as prints and posters in a variety of different sizes and styles. In the UK we also offer a range of other gift and stationery products illustrated with Frith photographs, although many of these are not available for delivery outside the UK – see our web site for more information on the products available for delivery in your country.

THE INTERNET

Over 100,000 photographs of Britain can be viewed and purchased on the Frith web site. The web site also includes memories and reminiscences contributed by our customers, who have personal knowledge of localities and of the people and properties depicted in Frith photographs. If you wish to learn more about a specific town or village you may find these reminiscences fascinating to browse. Why not add your own comments if you think they would be of interest to others? See **www.francisfrith.com**

PLEASE HELP US BRING FRITH'S PHOTOGRAPHS TO LIFE

Our authors do their best to recount the history of the places they write about. They give insights into how particular towns and villages developed, they describe the architecture of streets and buildings, and they discuss the lives of famous people who lived there. But however knowledgeable our authors are, the story they tell is necessarily incomplete.

Frith's photographs are so much more than plain historical documents. They are living proofs of the flow of human life down the generations. They show real people at real moments in history; and each of those people is the son or daughter of someone, the brother or sister, aunt or uncle, grandfather or grandmother of someone else. All of them lived, worked and played in the streets depicted in Frith's photographs.

We would be grateful if you would give us your insights into the places shown in our photographs: the streets and buildings, the shops, businesses and industries. Post your memories of life in those streets on the Frith website: what it was like growing up there, who ran the local shop and what shopping was like years ago; if your workplace is shown tell us about your working day and what the building is used for now. Read other visitors' memories and reconnect with your shared local history and heritage. With your help more and more Frith photographs can be brought to life, and vital memories preserved for posterity, and for the benefit of historians in the future.

Wherever possible, we will try to include some of your comments in future editions of our books. Moreover, if you spot errors in dates, titles or other facts, please let us know, because our archive records are not always completely accurate—they rely on 140 years of human endeavour and hand-compiled records. You can email us using the contact form on the website.

Thank you!

For further information, trade, or author enquiries
please contact us at the address below:

**The Francis Frith Collection, Frith's Barn, Teffont,
Salisbury, Wiltshire, England SP3 5QP.**

Tel: +44 (0)1722 716 376 Fax: +44 (0)1722 716 881
e-mail: sales@francisfrith.co.uk **www.francisfrith.com**